Love is...a dog's view through candid photos

Wendy Worthington

Love is...

As an animal lover literally hundreds of dogs (two of my own and the rest neighborhood friends') have come into my life and taken a piece of my heart with them when they left. Many of these dogs have since passed, but not before teaching me a great deal about love. I am forever grateful for the lessons!
Wendy Worthington

wendyworthington.com

Copyright © 2011 Wendy Worthington

Declarations

Published by
Anything For Money
In honor of Bruno Worthington, the sweetest Pomeranian that ever lived!

ISBN 978-0-615-45381-1

Love is...a dog's view through candid photos
wendyworthington.com

Love is sometimes in a tiny package

Love is sometimes huge

Love is cuddling as much as possible

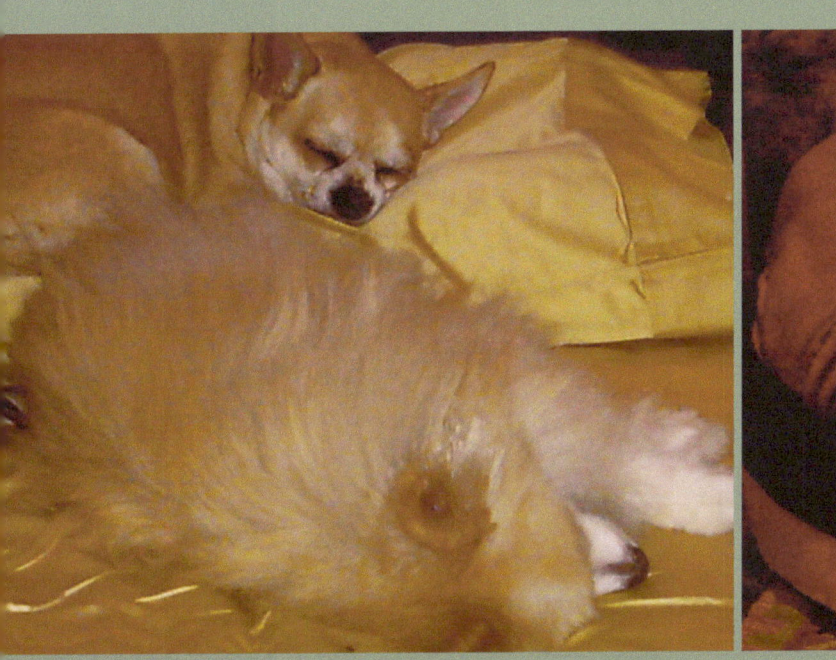

Love is hanging out with friends

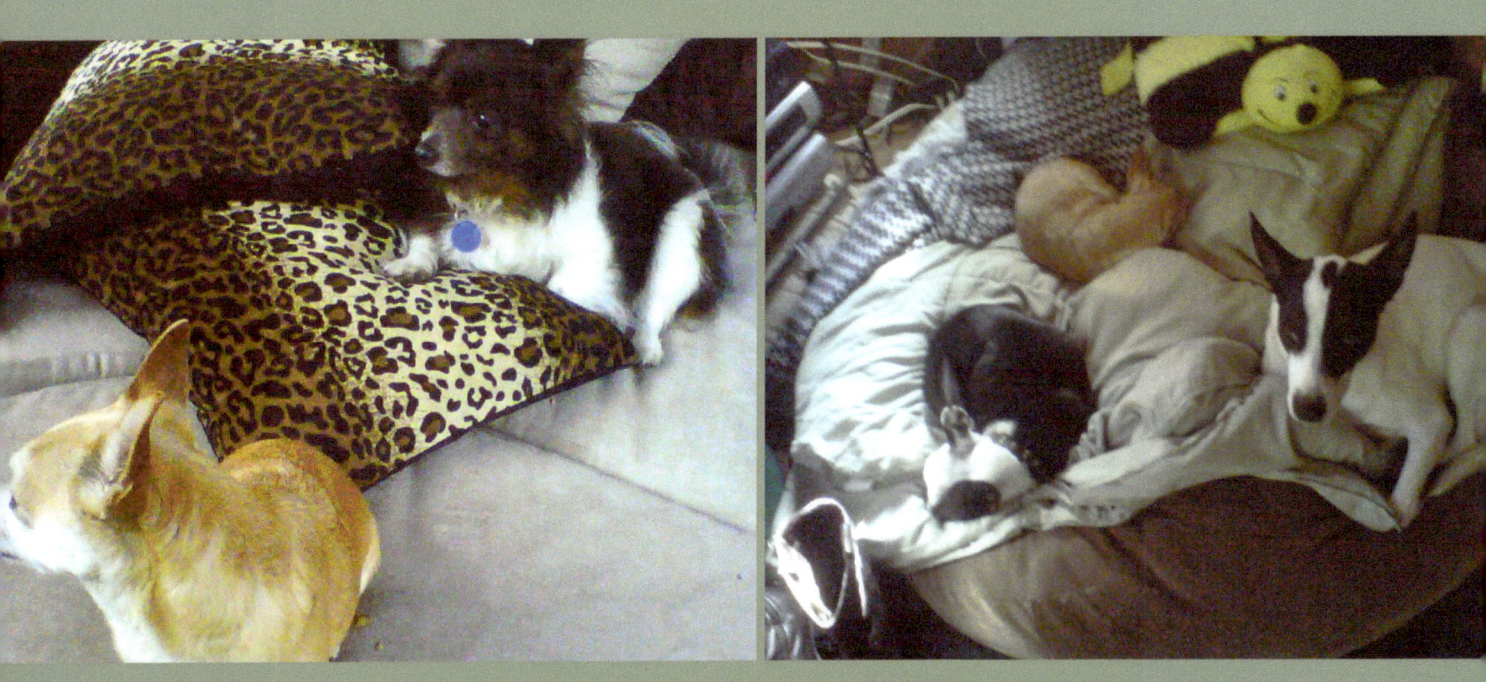

Love is showing interest in others

Love is sharing against your will

Love is always listening

Love is sometimes sacrificing pride

Love is finding every available moment in the sun

Love is knowing when
to look away

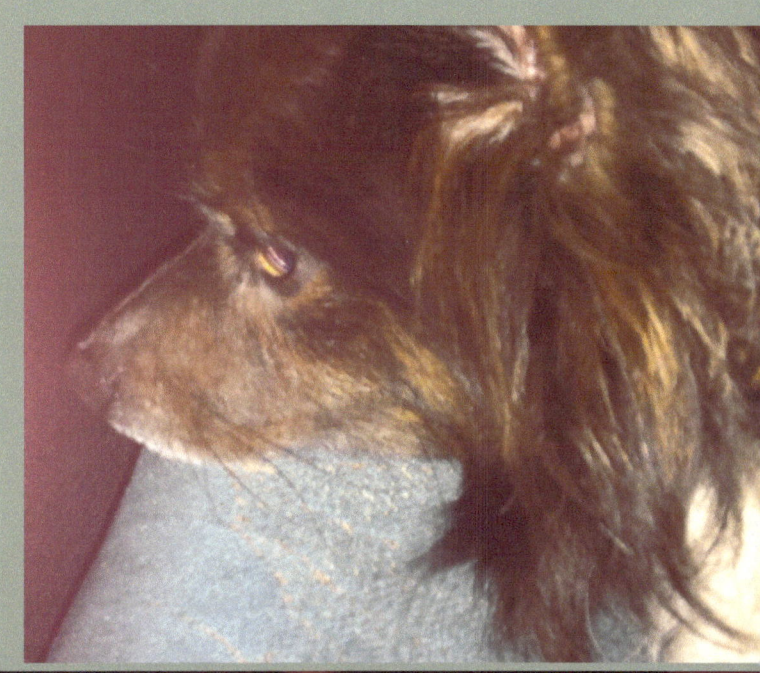

Love is defending territory

Love is looking
into the soul

Love is exhausting

Love is finding time to laugh

Love can be
confusing

Love is blind

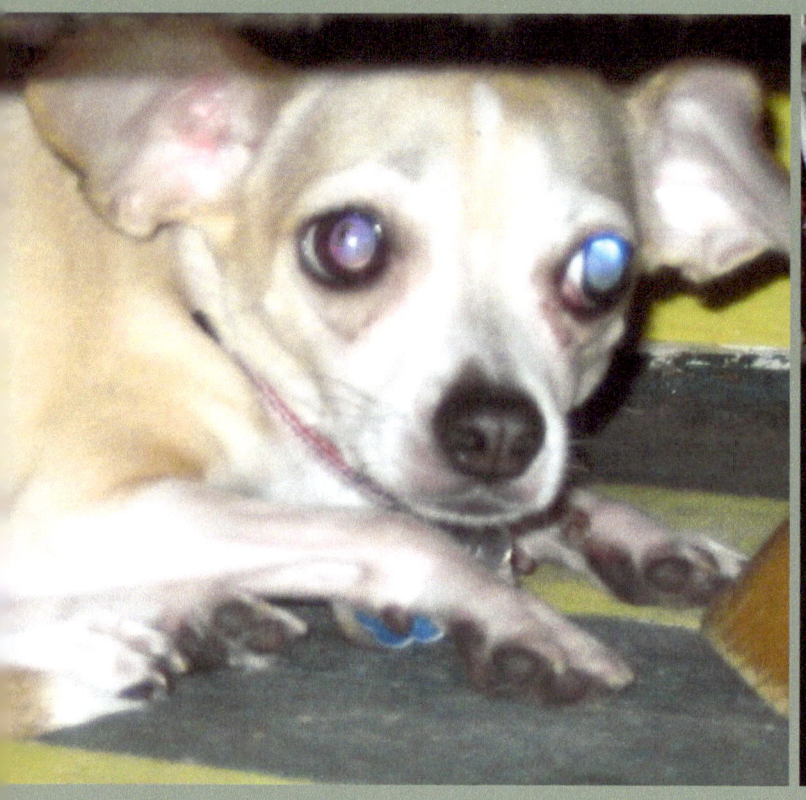 

Love can be scary

Love is sometimes sad

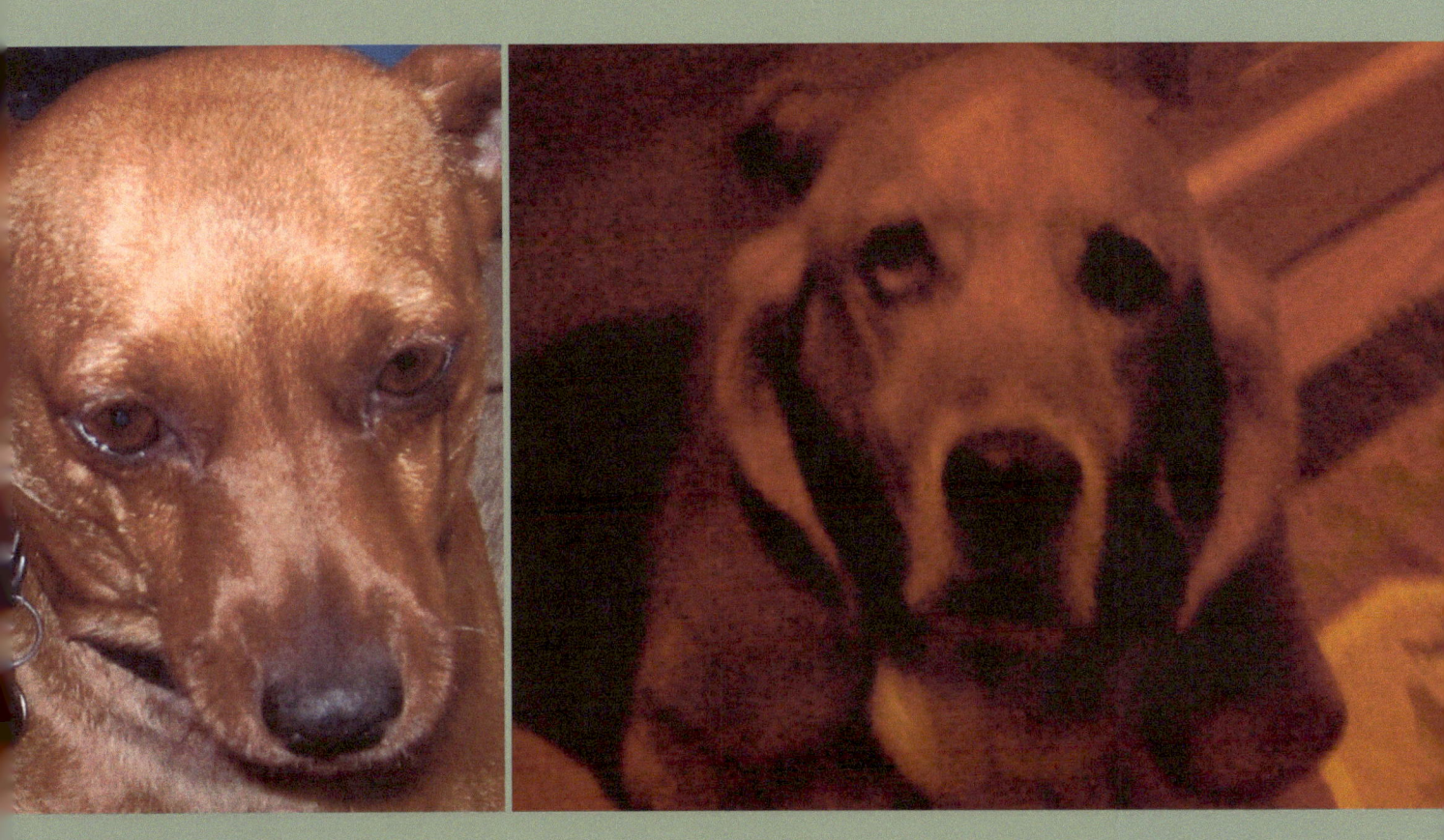

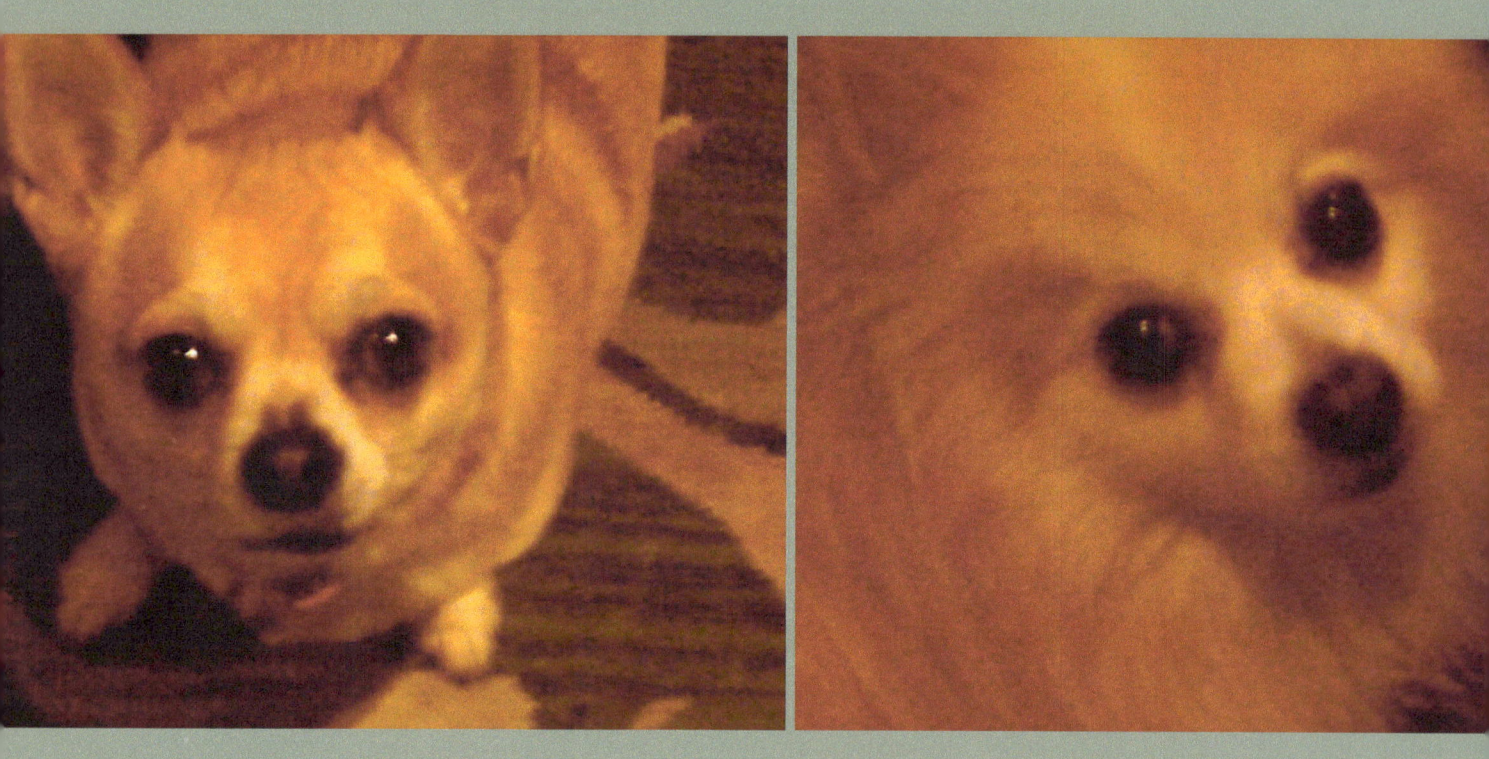

Love is sometimes irritable

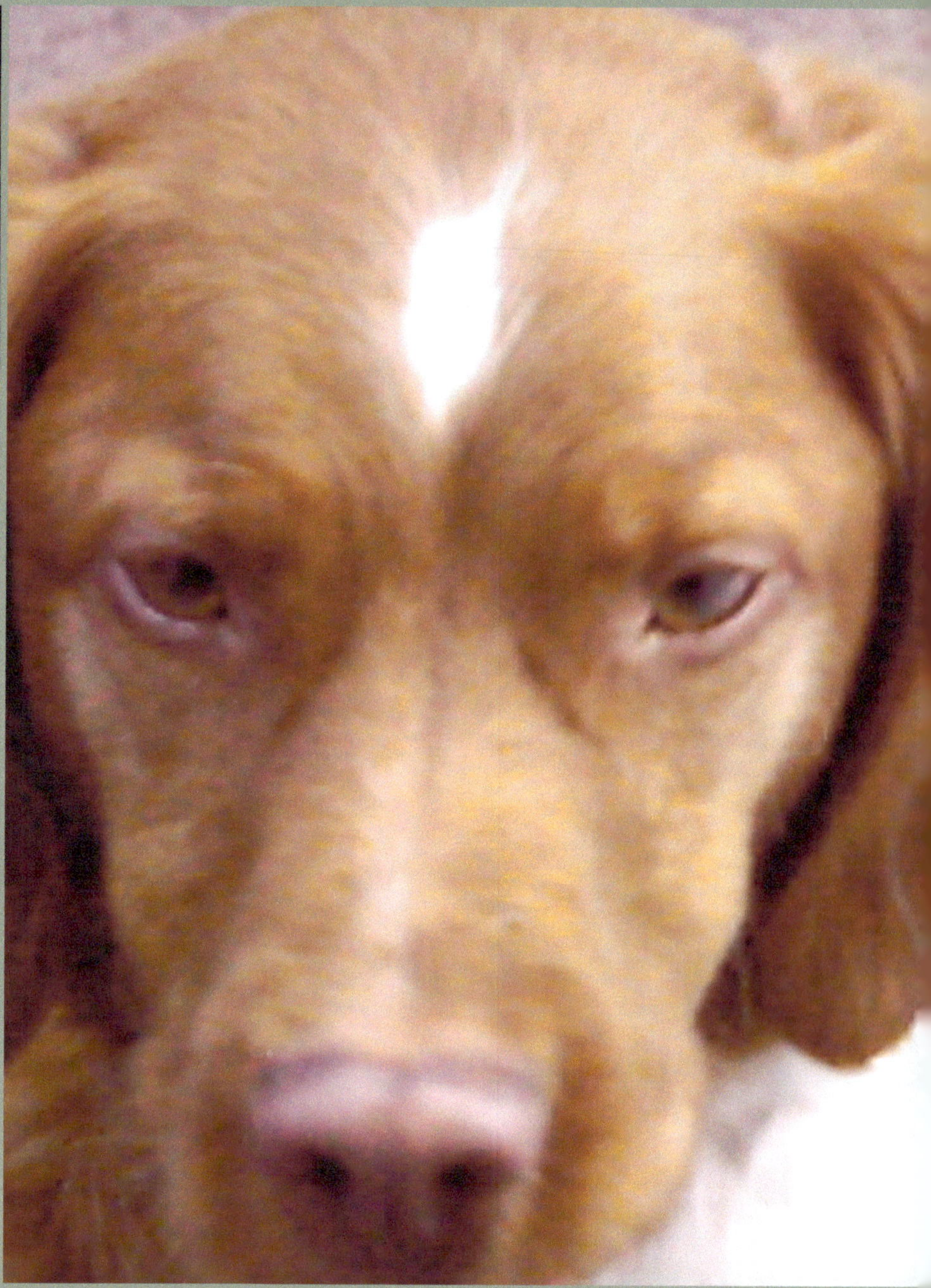

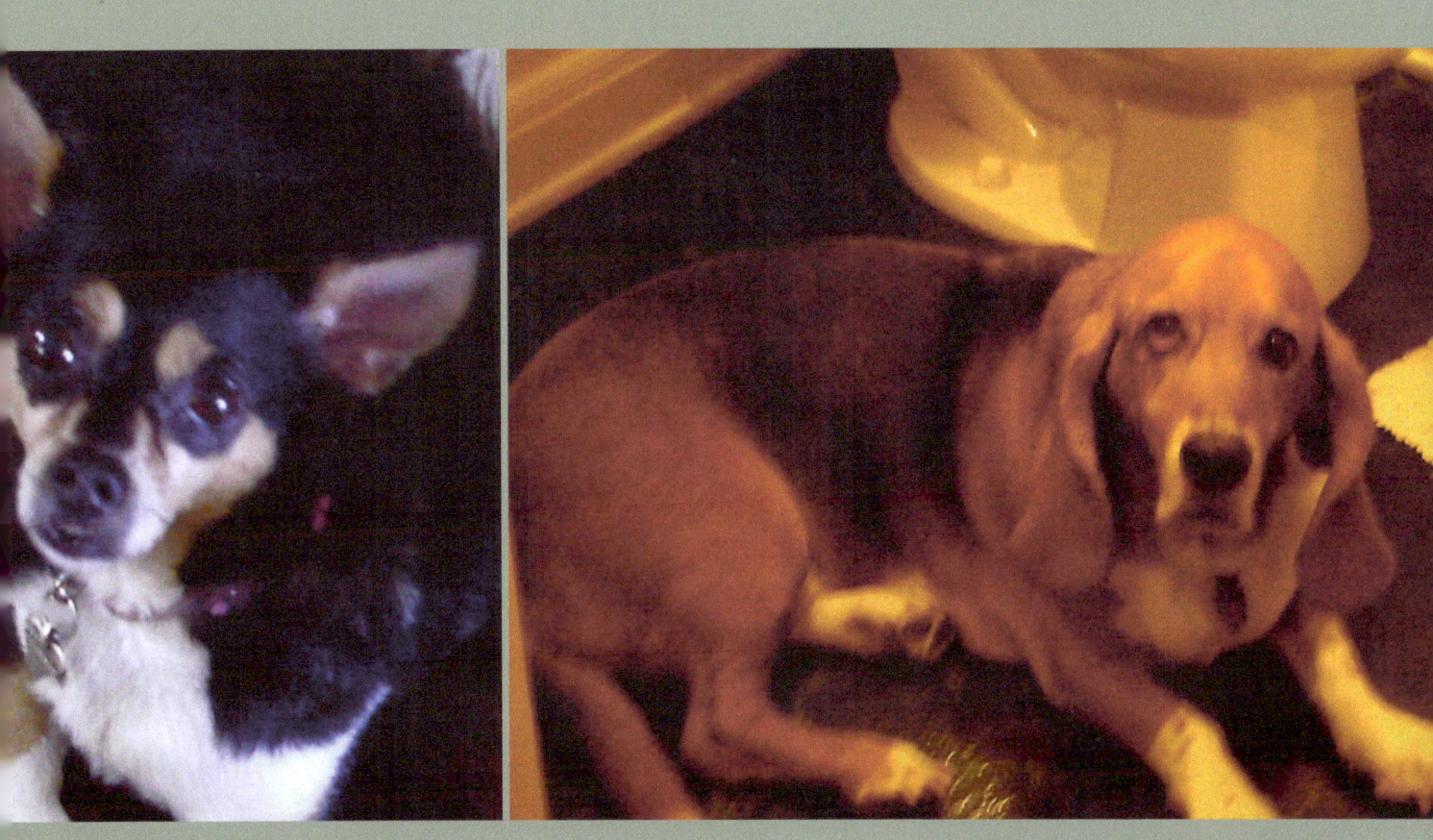

Love needs time
for reflection

Love is...a dog's view through candid photos

Wendy Worthington Anything For Money
wendyworthington.com
back cover photo of Bruno and Wendy Worthington by Mary Cellini